Farley the Red Panda

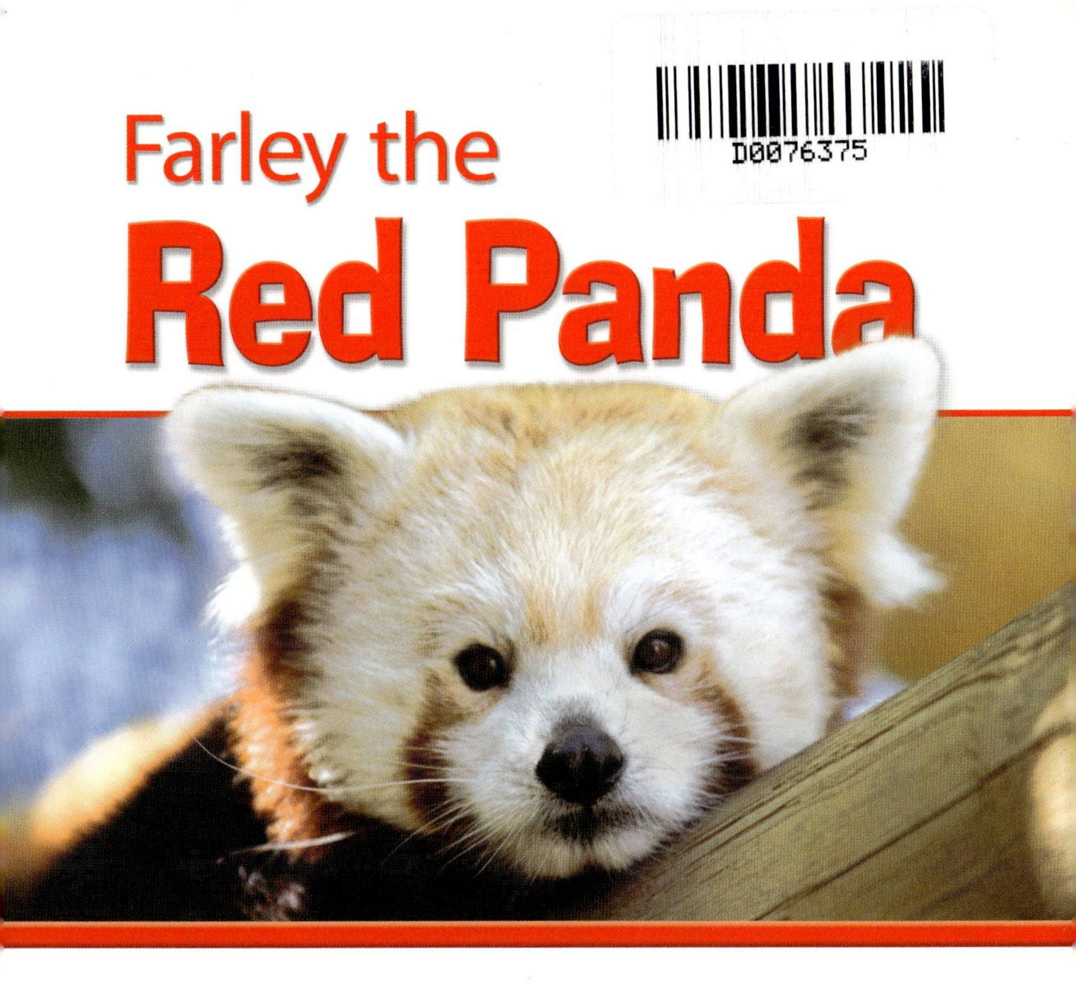

Rob Waring, *Series Editor*

Australia • Brazil • Japan • Korea • Mexico • Singapore • Spain • United Kingdom • United States

Words to Know

This story is set in the United States (U.S.). It happens in San Diego, California, and in a city called Syracuse [sirəkyus] in the state of New York.

A **At the Zoo.** Read the paragraph. Then complete the sentences with the underlined words.

This story begins at the San Diego Zoo. There are many animals that people can see at the zoo. However, this story is about a special red panda named Farley [fɑrli]. When Farley was born at the zoo, the zookeepers took him to be with other young animals at the nursery. There, Farley was raised by hand. Human beings, or people, gave him food and helped him from the time he was very young.

1. __________ are the people who care for animals at a zoo.
2. A __________ is a place for very young animals or children.
3. A __________ is a place where animals are kept and people go to look at them.
4. An animal that is __________ is cared for by people, not other animals.
5. A __________ is an animal that is slightly larger than a cat.

A Red Panda

B Animal Hospital.

Here are some words you will find in the story. Match each word with the correct definition.

1. hospital _____	**a.** something that is put into the body with a needle
2. sick _____	**b.** a special photograph that shows inside of the body
3. medicine _____	**c.** a substance that makes people healthy when they are unwell
4. X-ray _____	**d.** not healthy; unwell
5. injection _____	**e.** give food through a tube
6. tube feed _____	**f.** a place to take unhealthy people or animals for help

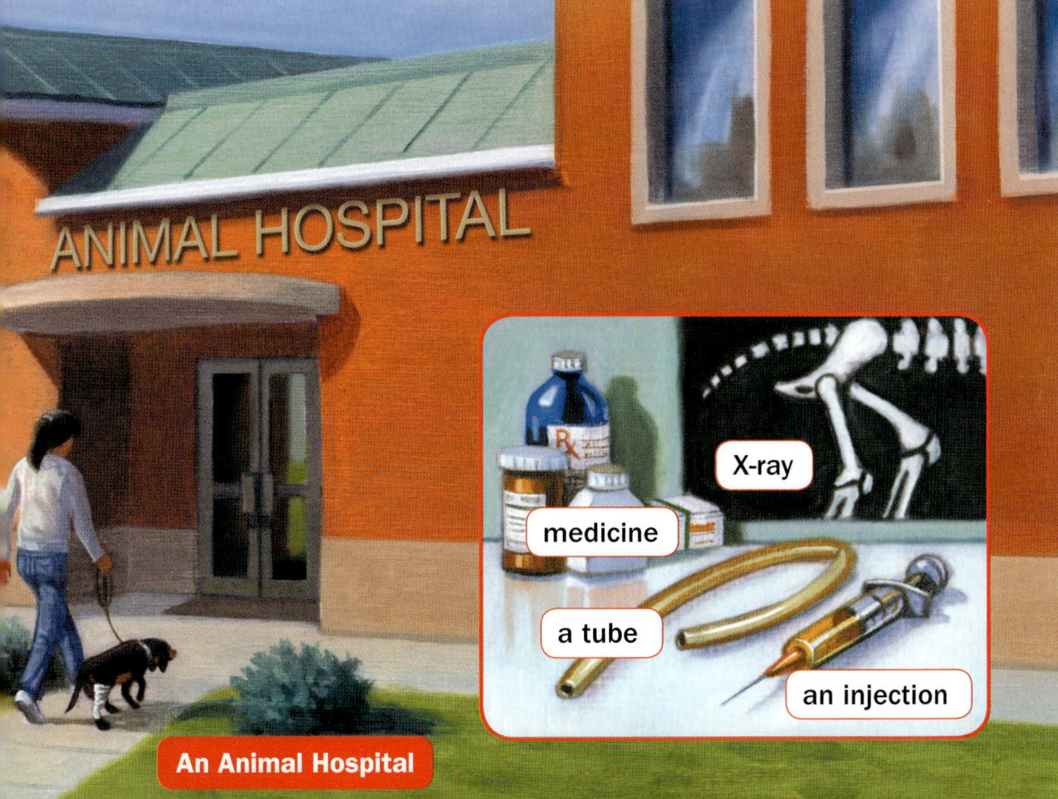

An Animal Hospital

Meet Farley. Farley is more than just a lovable red panda. He's also a fighter! Farley was born at the San Diego Zoo. He was his mother's first baby. Unfortunately, she wasn't able to take care of him when he was born. Zookeepers found him when he was only a few hours old. He was cold, **dirty**,[1] hungry, and alone.

The zookeepers were very worried about Farley, so they took him to the nursery at the zoo. One of the zookeepers describes his condition upon arrival. "When we first got a look at Farley, we were mostly concerned about two things: his early poor **nutrition**[2]—he had not been fed by the mother—and the fact that he was hypothermic, or had a low body **temperature**."[3]

It was clear to everyone that Farley was in trouble.

---

[1]**dirty:** not clean

[2]**nutrition:** the foods that are taken into the body and their effects on health

[3]**temperature:** how hot or cold something is

 CD 1, Track 01

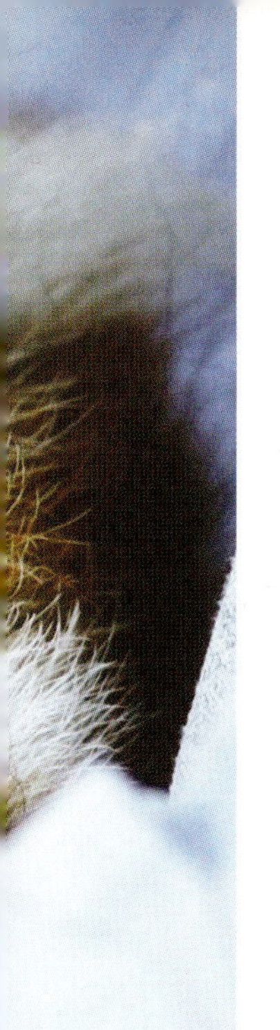

At the time, nursery workers didn't have much experience raising red pandas by hand. Farley was their first. However, they soon discovered how to do it successfully.

One nursery worker talked about Farley's time in the nursery. According to her, it was difficult at first—and a little **nerve-wracking**![4] But soon everyone in the nursery was pleased with Farley's improved health. Everything seemed to be going very well for him. But unfortunately Farley's problems weren't over yet.

---

[4]**nerve-wracking:** difficult to do and causing worry for the people involved

When he was only three weeks old, Farley stopped eating as much as he usually did. He couldn't **breathe**[5] very easily, either. The zookeepers took him to the zoo's hospital immediately. Farley had a very bad infection in his body and he was very sick. He was fighting for his life! For some time, it was uncertain if Farley would live or die.

[5]**breathe:** take air into the body

Infer Meaning

What does the word 'infection' mean? Look at the words around it on page 8. Then, write a definition for the word. Check your definition with your teacher or a dictionary.

Farley had to have many weeks of strong medicines and tube feedings. The nursery workers visited Farley every day. With the medicine and lots of care, he slowly got better. After he was in the hospital for a while, the zookeepers began to wonder: is Farley happy? Will all the hospital treatments affect him? After all of this, what kind of character will the little red panda have?

"We kept thinking, what's he going to be like?" reports zookeeper Janet Hawes. "The injections, the tube feedings, the X-rays, the hospital visits..." In the end, they were very pleased with the results. "What came out was just this darling little guy—he was a **doll**!"[6]

---

[6]**doll:** lovable; happy and friendly

After his long stay in the hospital, Farley was finally well enough to move back to his home at the nursery. That's where he's now working on taking his next step—learning to do the things that young red pandas do. One of the nursery workers reports, "The stage we're in right now is just to try to get him to be a better **climber**.[7] He's doing really well **exploring**."[8]

However, it seems Farley's travels aren't over. He has another surprise coming up!

---

[7] **climb:** use the legs, or legs and hands, to move the body up or down on something

[8] **explore:** go around and look for new things

Farley is now going to travel across the country to another zoo in Syracuse, New York. “Good morning, Farley!” says Janet Hawes as she walks into Farley’s room. “Today’s the big day. How are you feeling?”

Janet and the other zookeepers are a little sad, but they know that he has to go. “Although we’ll be very sad to say goodbye to Farley,” she says, “he’s been just a great, great experience for us. We know he needs more now than we can give him.”

What does Farley need? He needs to be around other red pandas. And at the Syracuse Zoo, Farley can finally get what he needs.

Meet Banshee. Banshee is another red panda. He was raised by hand in the Syracuse Zoo. He's about three weeks younger than Farley. According to zookeepers, it's very important for young red pandas to have other red pandas around them. "It's very important for red pandas as youngsters to have **playmates**[9] so that they don't **bond**[10] so completely with human beings," one zookeeper explains.

The zookeepers at Farley's new home in Syracuse are happy. They feel the new relationship between the two red pandas is a success. One of them explains, "As you can see, they're really active and they really like each other's company. And they like to play and sleep together now."

[9] **playmate:** a partner that one plays with often
[10] **bond:** form a relationship with someone or something

Back at the San Diego Zoo, Janet Hawes still remembers Farley and how special he was. She explains that Farley was special because he was such a fighter. He fought very hard to live and this fight helped to form his character.

For Janet, Farley was surprisingly friendly and loving, despite the difficult time he had in the beginning. Farley never stopped trying, even though things were very difficult. Janet seems very pleased by what a wonderful animal Farley has become. In fact, she thinks Farley the red panda is a really '**great guy**'![11]

---

[11]**great guy:** friendly term for a good or likeable person

Summarize

Imagine that you are a newspaper or radio reporter. Write or tell Farley's story. Include the following information:

1. How did he start his life?

2. What happened when he got sick?

3. Where is he now?

After You Read

1. On page 4, the word 'fighter' describes an animal that:
A. is in trouble
B. tries hard to succeed
C. is dangerous
D. argues often

2. Which was NOT one of Farley's problems when he was found?
A. poor nutrition
B. hypothermia
C. hunger
D. too hot

3. Why was it nerve-wracking for the nursery workers at first?
A. They had never seen a red panda.
B. Farley was too small.
C. They had never raised a red panda by hand.
D. Farley didn't like to eat.

4. When he was __________ one month old, Farley got a bad infection.
A. less than
B. already
C. over
D. more than

5. On page 11, 'we' in paragraph two refers to:
A. the zoo visitors
B. the red pandas
C. the zookeepers and nursery workers
D. Janet Hawes

6. Janet Hawes thinks that Farley is:
A. unhappy about the treatment
B. a sweet, friendly animal
C. very disagreeable
D. too afraid to be nice

7. Which is NOT a good heading for page 12?

A. Farley Gets a Surprise
B. Farley Moves Back to Nursery
C. Farley Is a Great Climber
D. No More Travels for Farley

8. What happens to Farley?

A. He moves from San Diego to Syracuse.
B. He goes to live with other red pandas.
C. He moves to a new zoo.
D. all of the above

9. In paragraph 1 on page 15, 'big' means:

A. important
B. active
C. large
D. real

10. How does Janet feel about saying goodbye to Farley?

A. unhappy and worried
B. afraid and worried
C. sad and happy
D. afraid and happy

11. Red pandas __________ bond too much with humans.

A. can't
B. must not
C. won't
D. must

12. What is the main lesson of this story?

A. Fighting for success builds character.
B. Pandas like being alone.
C. Difficult times are impossible.
D. Red pandas are just like people.

Jobs in Animal Care

Do you love animals? Do you think people must help and protect animals just like humans? Do you want to spend your days helping animals? If you answered 'yes' to any of these questions, maybe you should consider a job in animal care!

ANIMAL RIGHTS OFFICER:

Animal rights officers make sure that people treat animals properly. They visit homes, places where animals are bought and sold, zoos, and animal hospitals. They check to make sure that the places are clean, that the animals are getting proper nutrition, and that they have enough space to climb around and explore. Sometimes an animal rights officer will appear in court to protect the rights of an animal.

Animal Control Officers Help Animals in Danger

A Small Animal Doctor

ANIMAL CONTROL OFFICER:

To be an animal control officer, you must be in very good health because the job is an active one. Sometimes it involves getting animals out of dangerous situations, which can be nerve-wracking. For example, it's not always easy to get a cat down from a tree. Other times, animal control officers must take a sick animal to the hospital for treatment. These animals are often in great pain, and are afraid and difficult to control.

ANIMAL DOCTOR:

An animal doctor is called a 'veterinarian.' Some veterinarians work for zoos or animal hospitals. Others, often called 'small animal doctors,' treat smaller animals like dogs and cats. Many have their own private offices. Veterinarians do most of the same things doctors do. They take the animal's temperature, give injections, and take X-rays. They also decide what kind of medicine a sick animal may need. If an animal weighs too little, the doctor may use a feeding tube to make sure it gets enough nutrition. It takes six to seven years of higher education to become a doctor of veterinary medicine.

CD 1, Track 02

Word Count: 316
Time: _____

Vocabulary List